# For Children of All Ages

By
Sarah Jane Raffety

Copyright © 2017 Sarah Jane Raffety
Copyright © 2017 TEACH Services, Inc.
ISBN-13: 978-1-4796-0341-1 (Paperback)
ISBN-13: 978-1-4796-0342-8 (iBooks)
ISBN-13: 978-1-4796-0342-8 (Kindle Fire)
Library of Congress Control No: 2016919219

TEACH Services, Inc.
PUBLISHING
www.TEACHServices.com • (800) 367-1844

**O God,**

you have taught me from my
earliest childhood,

and I constantly tell others about
the wonderful things you do.

Now that I am old and gray, do
not abandon me, O God.

Let me proclaim your power to
this new generation,

your mighty miracles to all who
come after me"

(Ps. 71:17, 18, NLT).

To the three children dearest to my heart, Shelley, Michael, and Andrea, and to my husband Clyde:

Thank you, each one, for your supportive words and help along the way.

You have given so much to this book through your encouragement and love.

You fill me with happiness.

**O**nce upon a nighttime long ago, under the light of an unusual star, a tiny baby boy was born. It was a miraculous birth. He was a miracle baby.

They called Him Jesus.

"For unto us a Child is born, unto us a Son is given; and the government will be upon His shoulder" (Isa. 9:6).

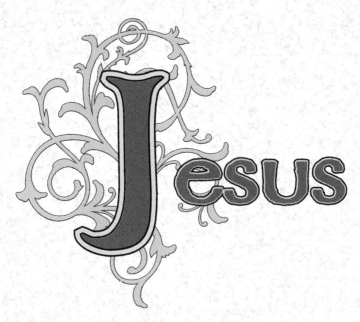

**Jesus**

delighted in the created world, where He heard the voice of Father God in heaven, speaking through its wonders.

Creation gently whispered messages of love, filled with knowledge and wisdom.

"For since the creation of the world His invisible attributes are clearly seen, being understood by the things that are made, even His eternal power and Godhead" (Rom. 1:20).

**G**od's

light and love shone upon Jesus. His mother held Him on her lap and told Him stories of God and His people from the ancient Holy Writings. He listened with deep interest, as though He had been there Himself.

"Your word is a lamp to my feet and a light to my path"
(Ps. 119:105).

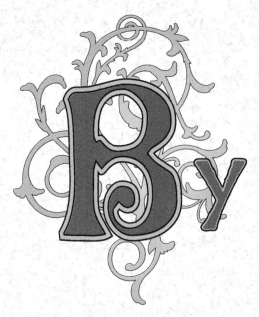

the age of twelve, Jesus' plain
understanding of God's word
astounded the priests, teachers,
and elders who had studied for
many, long years. He knew that
He had come from heaven to
fulfill God's loving purpose and
that He was God's own Son.

"I have more understanding than all my teachers, For Your testimonies are my meditation. I understand more than the ancients, Because I keep Your precepts" (Ps. 119:99, 100).

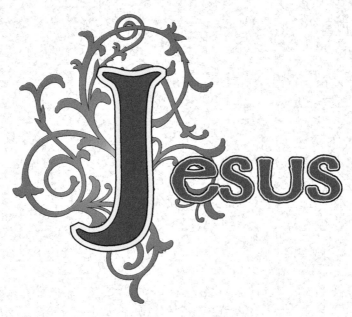

**Jesus**

grew up, working in his family's carpentry shop. As He worked, His spirit listened to His Father God in heaven. He increased in inner strength, faith, and power, and God revealed to Jesus His special mission: to win this world back from sin and death and return it to the kingdom of God.

"For I have come down from heaven, not to do My own will, but the will of Him who sent Me" (John 6:38).

**W**hen it was time to begin His special mission, Jesus went to the river to be baptized, in full surrender to God's will. God the Father spoke from heaven saying, "This is My beloved Son, in whom I am well pleased." God sent His Spirit as a dove, which rested upon Jesus.

"Behold! My servant whom I uphold, My Elect One in whom My soul delights! I have put My Spirit upon Him" (Isa. 42:1).

**The** Spirit of God led Jesus into the wilderness, where he ate no food for many days. There, at His weakest moment, He came face to face with this world's greatest enemy, the devil, known as Satan, who holds the world in bondage to sin and death. Satan tried to deceive Jesus into giving up His special mission by tempting him to deny God as His Father. But Jesus resisted the devil, so the world could be rescued from evil and won back to God and eternal life.

"The thief does not come except to steal, and to kill, and to destroy. I have come that they may have life" (John 10:10).

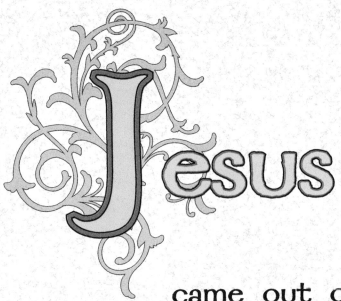

**J**esus came out of the wilderness victorious, filled with God's Holy Spirit, to begin His mission of teaching about the kingdom of God and how to have eternal life. He would minister by love alone, showing God's perfect and loving ways.

He chose certain men to stay close to Him, to teach them to become leaders in His work to save people. They were His disciples. There were twelve in all.

"Then Jesus said to them, 'Follow Me, and I will make you become fishers of men'" (Mark 1:17).

# Great

crowds followed after Jesus, just to catch His words, which brought life to their dry, sad spirits. Like seeds dropping into fertile ground, truth fell from His lips into poor, waiting hearts. There was never a greater teacher of the kingdom of God than Jesus, God's only Son.

"The words that I speak to you are spirit, and they are life"
(John 6:63).
"No man ever spoke like this Man!" (John 7:46).

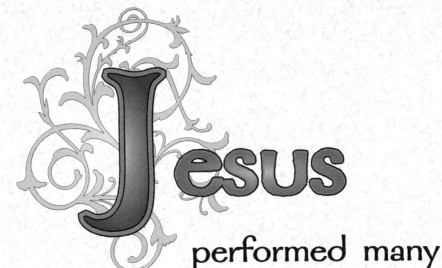

**J**esus performed many miracles, by which He lifted burdens and glorified His Father. The wind and sea calmed at His command. Plain water turned into delicious juice, and fish filled fishermen's empty nets, all at His word. He walked on the water, and He knew just where to tell His disciples to get money for their tax—out of the mouth of a fish! Nothing was too hard for Jesus.

"...many believed in His name when they saw the signs which He did"
(John 2:23).

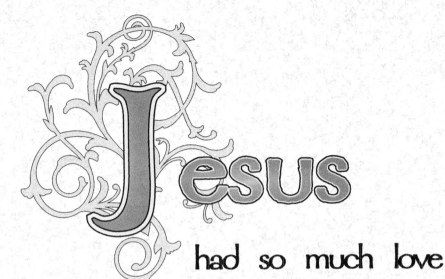

**Jesus**

had so much love for people. They came to him with all kinds of sickness and disease, and they brought their loved ones with them. He miraculously healed the deaf, the lame, the blind, and the sick. He released them from the grasp of demons. He increased a little boy's small lunch enough to feed a multitude of thousands. He forgave people their sins. His heart overflowed with love and kindness.

"Return to the LORD your God, for He is gracious and merciful, slow to anger, and of great kindness" (Joel 2:13).

**E**very

day God's Spirit of love worked through Jesus. Every day He spoke only the words of His Father God in heaven and did the miracles the Father gave Him power to do. What a surprise when people saw Him raise the dead to life! They discovered that Jesus even had power over death and the grave.

"Jesus said to her, 'I am the resurrection and the life. He who believes in Me, though he may die, he shall live'" (John 11:25).

# Satan

and those who did not love Jesus were jealous, so they plotted to kill Him. Jesus knew their thoughts. He had never done a sinful thing but had lived perfectly in every way, by the power of His Father. He also knew that He must give His own life to save this world and its people from sin and eternal death. Because of His great love for all people, He submitted to His Father's will and laid down His own life, as His cruel enemies nailed Him to a cross to die. The day was dark. Jesus suffered and died for you and me.

"For God so loved the world that He gave His only begotten Son, that whoever believes in Him should not perish but have everlasting life" (John 3:16).

**But** do you remember that Jesus has power over death? That's right! Though He died, the grave could not hold Him; He arose from the dead! He met with the disciples and instructed them to go to the whole world and teach all people to believe in Him for eternal life. He would go to heaven to work alongside the Father, preparing the way for believers to join them. He promised to come again to receive His people. The disciples watched as He rose up into heaven in a cloud.

"And if I go and prepare a place for you, I will come again and receive you to Myself; that where I am, there you may be also" (John 14:3).

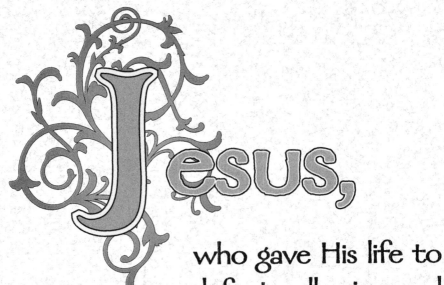

**Jesus,** who gave His life to defeat all sin and death, is alive in heaven right now, but He is also much closer than that. He sent His Holy Spirit to be with us here, as our helper, guide, and comforter. When you ask to be forgiven of your sins, Jesus, by His Spirit, comes right into your very heart to live. Jesus sees you, knows you, hears you, and loves you. You can talk to God anytime, anywhere, about anything, and He will never leave you nor abandon you.

Jesus is your best friend.

# Prayer of Invitation:

"Dear God,

Thank You for sending Jesus to die for me. I want to turn away from my sin and live my life in Your way. I accept Jesus as my Savior. Please forgive all of my sins and come into my heart to live. Help me to follow You always.

In Jesus' Name, Amen."

**A**t just the right time, not too soon, not too late, Jesus will come again. He will not come as a baby, as He did before. No, He will come as the King of kings and Lord of lords. The sky will open up, and every eye will see King Jesus and all His angels riding down on the clouds to the sound of great fanfare.

He will call to all His people in the graves, and they will arise. All believers who are alive will also hear His call and rise. His beloved people from every family, language, and nation will meet Jesus in the air to live with Him forever. Evil will be no more. Sin, sorrow, pain, and death will be finished.

Oh, wonderful day!!

"For the Lord Himself will descend from heaven with a shout, with the voice of an archangel, and with the trumpet of God. And the dead in Christ will rise first. Then we who are alive and remain shall be caught up together with them in the clouds to meet the Lord in the air. And thus we shall always be with the Lord" (1 Thess. 4:16, 17).

**A**ll of this is true, dear child. Read more about Jesus and His followers in the Bible, God's Holy Word. As you read the Bible and pray, you will grow strong, as Jesus grew. Believe in Him, for He is real. Trust Him completely. He is a faithful guide, and He knows the best way for you. He will shine His love on you and walk with you through all of your life.

Praise Him!

"The LORD bless you and keep you; the LORD make His face shine upon you, and be gracious to you; the LORD lift up His countenance upon you, and give you peace" (Num. 6:24–26).

**B**ut Jesus called them to Him and said, "Let the little children come to Me, and do not forbid them; for of such is the kingdom of God'" (Luke 18:16).

CPSIA information can be obtained
at www.ICGtesting.com
Printed in the USA
BVOW05s0924060617
R7994400001B/R79944PG485728BVX1B/1/P